Dinosaurs b

LONG-NECKED DINOSAURS

ANKING THEIR SPEED, STRENGTH, AND SMARTS

MARK WEAKLAND

BLACK
RABBIT
BOOKS

Bolt is published by Black Rabbit Books
P.O. Box 3263, Mankato, Minnesota, 56002.
www.blackrabbitbooks.com
Copyright © 2020 Black Rabbit Books

Jennifer Besel, editor; Catherine Cates,
interior designer; Grant Gould, cover designer;
Omay Ayres, photo researcher

Library of Congress Cataloging-in-Publication Data
Names: Weakland, Mark, author.
Title: Long-necked dinosaurs : ranking their speed, strength, and smarts /
by Mark Weakland.
Description: Mankato, Minnesota : Black Rabbit Books, [2020] | Series: Bolt.
Dinosaurs by design | Audience: Ages 8-12. | Audience: Grades 4 to 6. |
Includes bibliographical references and index.
Identifiers: LCCN 2018013946 (print) | LCCN 2018017058 (ebook) |
ISBN 9781680728316 (e-book) | ISBN 9781680728255 (library binding) |
ISBN 9781644660300 (paperback)
Subjects: LCSH: Dinosaurs—Juvenile literature.
Classification: LCC QE861.5 (ebook) | LCC QE861.5 .W3543 2020 (print) |
DDC 567.913—dc23
LC record available at https://lccn.loc.gov/2018013946

Printed in the United States. 1/19

Image Credits

CONTENTS

CHAPTER 1

GIANTS
on the Earth

The earth shakes. A small dinosaur looks up. That wasn't an earthquake. It's an enormous long neck stomping up the hill.

Long-necked dinosaurs were the largest animals to ever walk on Earth. No land animal living today gets close to the size of these giants.

COMPARING LENGTHS

Giant Plant Eaters

Long-necked dinosaurs were plant eaters. They used their necks to reach high branches and leaves. Legs like **pillars** supported their weight. Long tails helped them balance.

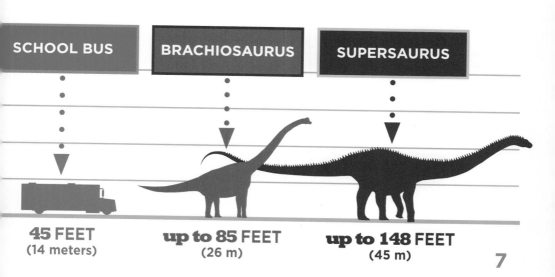

| SCHOOL BUS | BRACHIOSAURUS | SUPERSAURUS |

45 FEET (14 meters)   **up to 85 FEET** (26 m)   **up to 148 FEET** (45 m)

WHERE SOME LONG-NECKED DINOSAUR **FOSSILS** HAVE BEEN FOUND

MORRISON FORMATION
Apatosaurus
Brachiosaurus
Diplodocus
Supersaurus

ARGENTINA
Argentinosaurus
Saltasaurus

TANZANIA
Giraffatitan

URUGUAY
Saltasaurus

9

CHAPTER 2

Compare the

Apatosaurus

(uh-PAT-oh-sore-us)

This giant walked the forested **plains** of what is now North America. Each footstep must have shaken the ground.

This dinosaur's long tail ended in a thin tip. Some scientists think Apatosaurus might have used its tail like a **whip**. An earsplitting crack would scare off **predators**.

FEATURE FACTS

TOTAL LENGTH	**66 to 75 FEET** (20 to 23 M)	**NECK LENGTH** about **16 FEET** (5 M)
WEIGHT	up to **90,000 POUNDS** (40,823 KILOGRAMS)	

Years ago, scientists named both Apatosaurus and rontosaurus. They later decided they were the same animal. Today, Apatosaurus is the official name. But scientists are still studying the fossils. New research might prove they really are different animals.

Brachiosaurus

(BRAK-ee-uh-sor-us)

Brachiosaurus was about as long as a semitruck. And it weighed more than four elephants. Like all long necks, this dinosaur was strong. To fight, it might have hit an attacker with its long tail.

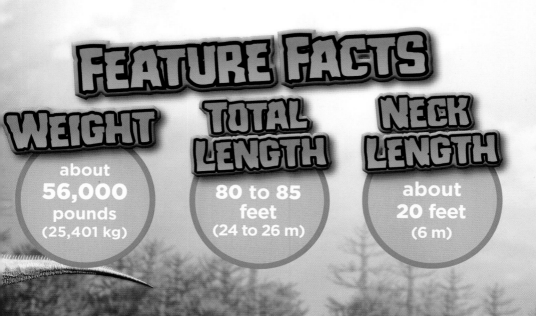

FEATURE FACTS

WEIGHT	TOTAL LENGTH	NECK LENGTH
about 56,000 pounds (25,401 kg)	80 to 85 feet (24 to 26 m)	about 20 feet (6 m)

Diplodocus

(dih-PLOD-uh-kus)

One of the first skeletons shown to the public was of Diplodocus. Like all long necks, this dino was probably slow moving. Scientists think its top speed was about 12 miles (19 kilometers) per hour.

FEATURE FACTS

TOTAL LENGTH 80 to 108 FEET (24 to 33 M)	**NECK LENGTH** about 26 FEET (8 M)
WEIGHT 20,000 to 56,000 POUNDS (9,072 to 25,401 KG)	

Long-necked dinosaurs didn't have good chewing teeth. Scientists think the animals swallowed big rocks. In the stomach, rocks tore apart plant food to help them **digest**.

Supersaurus

(SOO-per-sor-us)

Supersaurus was huge. It was so big, some scientists wonder if it had any predators. Meat eaters might not have been able to take down this big dino.

FEATURE FACTS

WEIGHT
up to
110,000
pounds
(49,895 kg)

TOTAL LENGTH
108 to 148
feet
(33 to 45 m)

NECK LENGTH
about
50 feet
(15 m)

Giraffatitan

(jih-RAFF-ah-ty-tan)

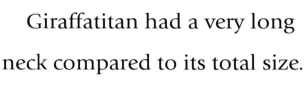

Giraffatitan had a very long neck compared to its total size. Scientists can't agree on how it, or other long necks, held their necks. Did they stretch them up high? Or did they hold their necks out straight? Held up, Giraffatitan's head would have been 40 feet (12 m) above the ground.

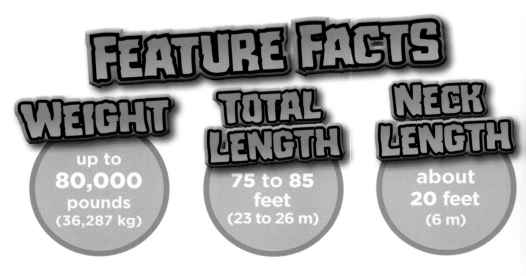

FEATURE FACTS

WEIGHT
up to
80,000
pounds
(36,287 kg)

TOTAL LENGTH
75 to 85
feet
(23 to 26 m)

NECK LENGTH
about
20 feet
(6 m)

Argentinosaurus

(ar-jen-TEEN-ah-sor-us)

Argentinosaurus belongs to a special group of long necks called titanosaurs. Titanosaurs had bony plates on parts of their bodies. The plates acted like **armor**.

FEATURE FACTS

WEIGHT
220,000 pounds
(99,790 kg)

TOTAL LENGTH
72 to 131 feet
(22 to 40 m)

NECK LENGTH
about 36 feet
(11 m)

THREE KINDS OF LONG-NECKED DINOSAURS

Long-necked dinosaurs can be placed into three groups. Each group has different features.

Diplodocids
(di-PLAH-da-sids)

very long tails
back legs longer than front legs

Titanosaurs
(ty-TAN-oh-sors)

armored with scales or bony plates

Brachiosaurids
(brak-ee-oh-SOR-ids)

extremely long necks front legs longer than back legs

Saltasaurus

(SALT-ah-SORE-us)

Saltasaurus was another titanosaur. Its fossils gave scientists the first proof titanosaurs had plates. Saltasaurus had bony growths on its back. They might have looked like spiky cones.

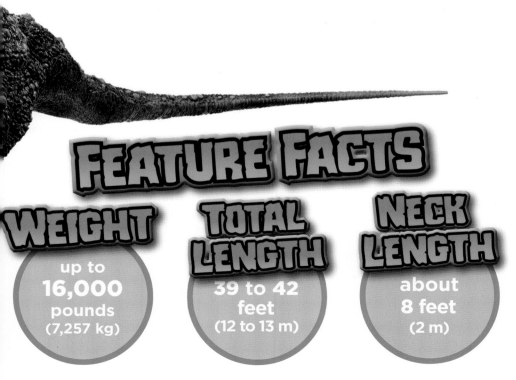

FEATURE FACTS

WEIGHT
up to
16,000
pounds
(7,257 kg)

TOTAL LENGTH
39 to 42
feet
(12 to 13 m)

NECK LENGTH
about
8 feet
(2 m)

CHAPTER 3

None Were

BIGGER

No land animals were ever bigger than the long-necked dinosaurs. These plant eaters walked slowly and were not very smart. Whipping their long tails helped keep predators away. But it was their enormous size that gave them the most protection.

COMPARE THEM!

Rank the dinos in this book. Then go find information on other long-necked dinos. How do they compare?

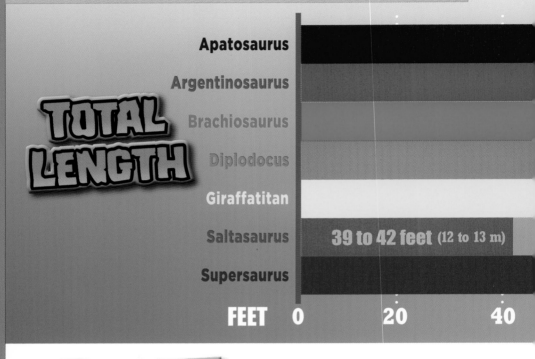

Apatosaurus	
Argentinosaurus	
Brachiosaurus	
Diplodocus	
Giraffatitan	
Saltasaurus	39 to 42 feet (12 to 13 m)
Supersaurus	

FEET 0   20   40

WEIGHT

Apatosaurus

up to
90,000 pounds
(40,823 kg)

Supersaurus

up to
110,000 pounds
(49,895 kg)

Argentinosaurus

up to
220,000 pounds
(99,790 kg)

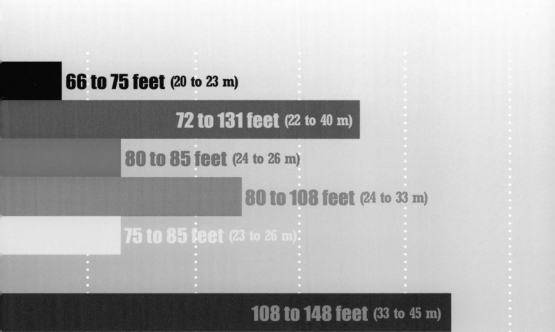

66 to 75 feet (20 to 23 m)

72 to 131 feet (22 to 40 m)

80 to 85 feet (24 to 26 m)

80 to 108 feet (24 to 33 m)

75 to 85 feet (23 to 26 m)

108 to 148 feet (33 to 45 m)

80   100   120   140   160

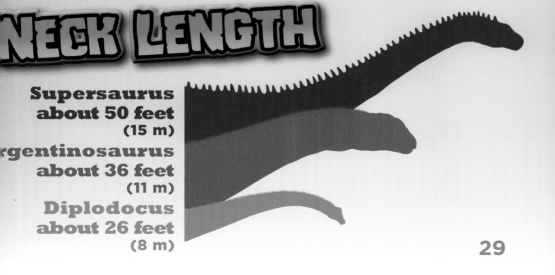

NECK LENGTH

Supersaurus
about 50 feet
(15 m)

rgentinosaurus
about 36 feet
(11 m)

Diplodocus
about 26 feet
(8 m)

armor (AR-muhr)—a protective outer layer

digest (DY-jest)—to change the food eaten into a form that can be used by the body

fossil (FAH-sul)—the remains or traces of plants and animals that are preserved as rock

pillar (PIL-uhr)—a firm upright support for a big structure

plain (PLAYN)—a stretch of nearly treeless country

predator (PRED-uh-tuhr)—an animal that eats other animals

whip (WHIP)—an instrument consisting usually of a handle and lash forming a flexible rod that is used for whipping

BOOKS

Gregory, Josh. *Brachiosaurus.* Dinosaurs. Ann Arbor, MI: Cherry Lake Publishing, 2016.

Peterson, Megan Cooley. *The Dinosaur Extinction: What Really Happened?* History's Mysteries. Mankato, MN: Black Rabbit Books, 2019.

West, David. *Long-Necked Dinosaurs.* Prehistoric Animals. New York: Windmill Books, 2016.

WEBSITES

Dinosaurs & Prehistoric
kids.nationalgeographic.com/animals/hubs/dinosaurs-and-prehistoric/

Dinosaurs for Kids
kidsdinos.com/dinosaurs-for-kids/

Prehistoric World
www.nationalgeographic.com/science/the-prehistoric-world/

INDEX